THE GHOSTLY TALES OF COLUMBIA

Published by Arcadia Children's Books
A Division of Arcadia Publishing
Charleston, SC
www.arcadiapublishing.com

Spooky America is a trademark of Arcadia Publishing, Inc.

First published 2023

Manufactured in the United States

ISBN 978-1-4671-9728-1

Library of Congress Control Number: 2023931841

All images used courtesy of Shutterstock.com.

Notice: The information in this book is true and complete to the best of our knowledge. It is offered without guarantee on the part of the author or Arcadia Publishing. The author and Arcadia Publishing disclaim all liability in connection with the use of this book.

Spooky America

THE GHOSTLY TALES OF COLUMBIA

KAREN EMILY MILLER

adapted from *Haunted Columbia, Missouri* by Mary Collins Barile

arcadia
CHILDREN'S BOOKS

MISSOURI

COLUMBIA

KANSAS

OKLAHOMA

IOWA

ARKANSAS

Table of Contents & Map Key

KENTUCKY

Welcome to Spooky Columbia!

Do you like spooks? I do, and that's why I love Columbia, Missouri. Here, ghosts and spirits spill out of the town and into the countryside. In fact, there are so many ghosts in this part of the country that they can't all fit in this book! Why are there so many of them? Maybe it's because of all of the old battlefields. Or perhaps the people of Missouri aren't afraid of spirits. In fact, some folks here even *welcome* ghosts.

Back in the 1800s and early 1900s, when disease and war took many before their time, Missouri was the center of the spiritualist movement. Back then, some people thought there were ways to communicate with the dead. After all, who wouldn't want to communicate with a loved one who has passed? To make sure they were at peace and in a place that made them happy? Many Missourians did. So they held séances—gatherings where people try to contact the spirit world.

Then, in 1890, Ouija (pronounced "wee-jee") boards were invented. That's a board with numbers and letters on it that people use to talk to spirits from beyond the grave. It was much more convenient to pull out a Ouija board than holding a séance … but it could still get super spooky!

The ghostly good news is, you won't need to go to a séance or use a Ouija board to discover some of Columbia's most famous spooks. In these pages, you'll meet the spinster ghost who doesn't like *anyone* peeking around her house. You'll relive a Civil War battle with the spirits. And you'll meet the (possibly haunted?) statue of John Neihardt himself, a pioneer in paranormal research. But that's just the spine-tingling start. Because there are *many* more waiting for you (and they've been waiting a while). So grab a spooky snack, cozy up by the campfire, and read on!

The Katy Tunnel

ROCHEPORT, MISSOURI

When you first moved to Rocheport, Missouri, you knew it was different than most other towns. (After all, have *you* ever lived in a place where they have blue bottle trees in backyards? They have them in Rocheport.)

These blue bottles have been stuck on branches for a few hundred years, ever since people thought they might protect against evil spirits who like to lurk at night. The bottles sway in the breeze alongside peonies and roses, and no one thinks it's odd.

A neighbor, a kid around your age, tells you why the bottles are special. Their color is cobalt blue, the color of a night sky. "Ghosts and spirits are afraid of blue," he explains. "Blue is the color of the sky. All that open space? That rattles the spirits!"

A wind blows into the garden, making some of the bottles moan with a low whistle.

"We're going to catch some spirits, just you see." The kid cracks a smile and points at the bottles. "Ghosts get so curious about the sound that they climb inside and get stuck. That's when we cork up the bottles and toss them."

Yup. Rocheport is definitely different from anywhere you've ever lived.

You ask, "What else is special about Rocheport?"

Your neighbor is only too happy to tell you. He begins by saying the town sits on the bank of the Missouri River, and that it's surrounded by limestone cliffs. "Water and limestone," he explains, "are *spook magnets*. Add the nearby Big Moniteau Cave, and you have a ghost hunter's dream destination." Then he tells you all about the mysterious paintings inside the cave. "They've almost faded away," he says, "but with a little imagination, you'll see a snake, a wild turkey, the sun, the moon, and more." He goes on to share that there are

creatures with horns, scales, and tails so long that they wind around the creatures' bodies, and that the local Indigenous peoples named the figures "manitou," or spirit creatures of the land. He grins. "Trust me. It's the *perfect* setting for something spooky."

You hope that's true as you take off for a bike ride along the Katy Trail, a favorite nature trail for locals. Once a railroad line, it became a recreational trail when the state pulled up the railroad ties and replaced them with gravel. The trail now stretches all the way across the state of Missouri.

You wonder why the old railroad tunnel scares people. You've always liked train tunnels. In fact, you've put pennies on the rails and waited for trains to roll by. They'd squash the coins into flat metal puddles. You wish the train still ran. You have a pocketful of pennies.

The sun is setting as you pull up to the tunnel.

Suddenly, all the other hikers and cyclists are gone. Maybe it's the light rain that has been falling for the last hour. Nobody likes getting wet.

Good thing I'm wearing my rain parka, you think as you pull up the hood. You also have a sturdy flashlight, a Swiss Army knife, and a compass—everything an adventurer needs.

The ground fog rolls in. This is thick, almost impenetrable fog, not like the gray, wet wisps you bike through on your way home from school. You click on your flashlight, but the fog acts like a mirror and shines the light back at you. You have to squint to see anything.

Then, strangely, you realize it's silent. Shouldn't you be able to hear something? Like the crunch of bike tires on gravel, or the sound of the rain?

You tell yourself you're not scared. Then you say it aloud, just to make sure you believe it. "I am *not* scared!" But your heart is beating faster now. You glance over your shoulder. It would be silly to turn around and retrace your steps. But if you go through the tunnel, you'll be back home in no time.

You wheel your bike into the tunnel, just a few yards. The railroad ties are long gone. The surface is smooth. You take a deep breath and go deeper into the tunnel. It's not that long, you remind yourself. You think you see a pinprick of light up ahead. You're almost there. Before you know it, you'll be on the other side.

But suddenly, like a scream in the night, a steam whistle blows, its pitch riding high, falling low. Your heart hammers in your chest. A train whistle? How could that be? There hasn't been a train in here for years.

Except then . . . you hear the *chug chug* of a train engine.

Your body floods with panic. *Run!* you tell

yourself. *Run now!* You drop your bike and dash down the tunnel trail. Is it your imagination, or do you really feel the ground vibrating below your feet? The sound is getting closer. The chugging fills your chest, the whistle pierces your ear drums. The train is almost here! You can't outrun it, so you press yourself flat against the tunnel wall and squeeze your eyes shut.

Suddenly, you feel a powerful rush of air, so strong it nearly knocks you down. And then . . . nothing.

Breathing hard, you rush to grab your bike. Your legs are shaking, but somehow you make it out of the tunnel. When you do, you find that the rain has stopped. The fog has disappeared, and once again you hear the crunch of bike tires on gravel.

That's when you spot a pair of bicyclists biking toward you on the trail. "*Wait!*" you call, waiving your hands so they'll stop. "Did you hear it? Did you hear the train?"

The cyclists—a man and woman—are both clearly trying to suppress a laugh. They think you are just another kid with a big imagination. Still, they answer your question.

"There hasn't been a train here since 1893," the woman says. "You've probably noticed there aren't any railroad ties, either."

You look back at the tunnel. A moment ago, you could have sworn you were running on railroad tracks, a massive train barreling down on you. But the cyclists are right, you realize. The tracks *are* gone. And below your feet, there's nothing but a gravel trail.

A shiver darts up your spine. Maybe that's all a ghost train needs.

You mutter a thank you, push off, and ride home. You promise yourself that next time— if there is a next time—you'll come here with a friend. Maybe that neighbor with the blue bottle tree has a bike.

CHAPTER 2

The Battle of Goslin Lane

WOODLANDVILLE, MISSOURI

During the Civil War, Missouri was torn between the North and the South. Woodlandville is in a part of Missouri that decided to fight for the North, or Union, side of the war. But there were still plenty of Confederate sympathizers (people who sided with the South) around. Wagon trains carrying supplies to the Union armies could expect attack, even when traveling in Union territory. That's exactly what happened on September 23, 1864.

A group of one hundred Confederate soldiers, including the notorious bank robbers Jesse and Frank James, fell upon the wagon train. The Confederates came on so fast that the Union soldiers didn't have time to form battle lines.

The Confederates showed no mercy to the Union soldiers. One observer said they screamed like wild men, whooping and yelling, "Wa-woo-woo-hoo!" as they tore into them. "A massacre," another said, "that ended only when darkness fell."

At the end of the day, ninety-two men lay dead. The Confederates stole food, ammunition, even blue Union uniforms. Why uniforms? The Confederates camouflaged themselves to confuse the North in a battle five days later.

History books describe what happened that day as a skirmish, a brief unplanned battle.

But those who witnessed it said it was much darker. Maybe that is why a sense of danger still hangs in the air at the battle site. Some say that when something terrible happens, the place where it happens doesn't forget, even though the people are long gone. You wonder if all those spooky memories are what make this place haunted.

"That's the story," your uncle says as you ride with him to the exact spot where the massacre took place.

"It must have been exciting," you say. "I wish I could have been there. I would have fought hard to protect my friends."

"You wouldn't have wanted to be there," your uncle says, shaking his head solemnly. "It was awful." He usually blasts music as he drives, but he turns off the radio. "You have to pay attention on this stretch of road," he says. "You might hear a truck's horn, but not see it until it's almost on top of you." He slows down, rolls down his window, and tells you to do the same.

When you complain that it's too cold to have the windows down, he says, "Just wait." After a while, a Civil War marker comes into view, and he pulls off the road next to it.

You both get out of the car. "Skirmish of Goslin Lane," you read on the sign.

He nods. "This is where it happened. Ninety-two men killed within hours."

You stand there, quiet, thinking about it. Then, somewhere to your left, you see a spark. Or is it a sparkle? A flash? You look across the road to the houses, but no one seems to be home. *That's odd*, you think. *Where is the light coming from?*

Your uncle nudges you and puts his hand to his ear. For a split second, you wonder if this whole thing is a joke. Your uncle has been known to play tricks. But then . . . you hear it.

Crack, crack . . . the sound of gunshots. You jump, startled. "What was *that*?" you whisper.

He doesn't answer and only motions for you to keep listening. You focus hard, but now it's quiet all over again. You were right, you realize. Your uncle's just trying to scare you. You're about to tell him to cut it out when a shrill cry echoes in the distance.

Whinny, neigh . . . the sound of horses in distress.

The breath catches in your throat. You scan the nearby woods, waiting for hunters to burst from the brush. But you still can't see anything.

All of a sudden, your uncle grabs your arm and pulls you off the road. There's a whirling cacophony of voices. Men shouting, screaming, hooting . . . it's terrifying.

"Wee-hoo-hoo!"

Your mouth drops open. It's the Confederate war cry!

Clop, clop, the sound of horses galloping toward you! The crack of a rifle.

Your heart pounds. Any moment they'll crest the hill. Will they shoot you, too?

You might be almost grown, but you don't shake off your uncle's arm as he tries to shield you from whatever is coming.

You brace yourself, but as quickly as it began, the storm of neighs and shouts and gun shots rolls over you. It heads off the road and vanishes like smoke into the hills.

"*Phew*," says your uncle, loosening his grip on you. "I wasn't expecting that."

"What do you mean?" For a split second, you wonder if maybe he's tricked you after all. "What were you expecting?"

"Well," he says, "I thought if we came out here today, we might see or hear something spooky."

He shakes his head. "I just wasn't expecting

something *that* spooky." He points to the Civil War marker next to us. "See the date?" he asks.

"September twenty-third," you read aloud. "Wait. That's *today*."

"Right." Your uncle nods. "Today is the anniversary of the massacre. It's also late afternoon, the same time the attack occurred."

Whoa.

You glance back at the wooded hills and shiver. You can't imagine all the things they've seen.

Your uncle crosses over to the truck and rolls up the windows. "No need to keep them open anymore."

You agree. You're still not entirely sure you believe in ghosts, but you've seen and heard enough today in Woodlandville to know that war is always horrible. Even if just the ghostly echo of one that happened long ago.

Haunted Hill

MEXICO, MISSOURI

Close your eyes for a moment and imagine a place so haunted that it's nicknamed "The Ghost District." Are you picturing a neighborhood of rundown Victorian mansions with signs that say "No Trespassing" posted in their front yards? If so, you're on the right track. But this ghost district is not found in the city. It's found along a lonely county road.

People say this place outside of Columbia is where spirits, creatures, and nightmares come to life.

The hauntings started in the fall of 1884. Nineteen years had passed since neighbor fought neighbor and cousins battled cousins during the Civil War. After years of battle and bloodshed, peace had finally come and the city had started to thrive. The railroad had arrived in town, a women's college and music conservatory attracted talented young people, and the population boomed.

But in 1884, everything changed. What happened that year to break the peace? Something, or *somethings* woke up. That year, the number of spirits reported almost matched the number of people who said they saw them.

At first, the spirits only frightened horses. This, of course, affected the people who rode them. Locals enjoying themselves on carriage rides, farmers taking crops and livestock to market, and even lone travelers all reported that something spooked their horses when they came to a certain hill. Some of the horses foamed at the mouth, others reared and bucked. There were so many wrecks that pieces of buckboards and buggies littered the ravines alongside the road.

That first year, a nearby farmer claimed there had been almost fifty accidents because of spooked horses. Investigators checked the road for potholes, which were known to scare horses. However, the road was in good shape; better than other roads in the county.

Little by little, the hill and its spirits became famous around town. One resident even wrote a poem about the hauntings.

"A deep ravine on either side,
The gnarled and scrubby oaks divide
Where hooting owls' dark ills betide it.
It seems a place where fiends abide."

The paranormal activity started in September, just after the first frost. It lasted all winter. People claimed to hear frightening moans and shrieks coming from the hill itself. Ghost hunters promised to catch whatever being haunted the hill. But each night as they stood guard, they heard nothing but the hoots of owls.

The attacks continued. One man said a creature attacked him and stole his horse. Another time, when the young ladies from the music conservatory wanted a break from their studies, they filled a buggy with friends and traveled to the hill. Later, the only thing they remembered was being thrown from their carriage after the horses spooked. After that incident, everyone avoided the hill at night, at least until spring, when the days grew longer. Whatever was haunting the hill might be better avoided if you could see it coming.

As time went on, strange things began to happen in and around town. When cows moaned and dogs howled, townspeople blamed the nearby hill. When a field burst suddenly into flames, they said it was caused by the spirit of the hill.

Did anyone actually see a spook? Most agreed they had seen a man dressed in black. He seemed to be able to slip in and out of shadows. He'd appear suddenly in front of the horses, fix his stare on them, then vanish as quickly as he had appeared. Once, a rider stopped on the hill after hearing a woman wail. He tethered his horse to a tree and went to look. He didn't find her.

What he did find was trouble. A pair of glowing eyes popped up next to him. Bony hands grabbed at his jacket and throat.

Some thought the haunting was a result of a local killing. The story went that a local girl had angered her outlaw father when she took up with one of the members of his gang. The father was not happy. Then he decided that her young man was cheating the gang. Declaring him a traitor, the father drew his gun to kill him. The girl is said to have stepped in front of her lover just when the father's gun went off. Was she the one who passersby heard crying?

Blaming the hauntings on the unfortunate girl didn't explain the sightings of the wild man or the moans from inside the hill. A better explanation might have come from the local newspapers. After investigating the paranormal incidents, reporters encountered an interesting man.

John Creasy had lived near the haunted hill for many years. People said he bought the hill as a money-making venture. He wanted to charge travelers ten cents for a look at a cave close to the hill. He said a spirit hid out in the cave's interior. If the visitors were lucky, they might catch a peek at what was haunting the hill.

One brave visitor said he saw a phantom float over the mouth of the cave. He claimed that when he peered inside the cave, he saw a corpse candle. A corpse candle is a frightening sight. It's a glow that's seen even though there's no candle.

Thankfully, five years after the hauntings began, they ended. However, if you're ever driving near the Ghost District of Mexico, Missouri, and you see a "detour" sign, maybe you should turn around. Maybe the haunted hill has awoken!

CHAPTER 4

Farmhouse Haunting

COLUMBIA, MISSOURI

Columbia is a town full of spirits. It seems like everyone has a story to tell. When you're at the Farmer's Market one Saturday, you hear a new tale. It almost leads you on a wild ghost chase.

Your family pauses at a stand that sells tomatoes. They're ripe—so ripe you can almost taste the sweet tanginess. Maybe because you bought a whole bag, or maybe because she has never met a stranger, your mom strikes up a conversation with the farmer who sold you the tomatoes.

"I'm from a farm just outside of town," the farmer says. "It's been in our family since before the Civil War. It's hard work, but we're proud to be farmers." She sighs. "I don't live there anymore, though. I'm off the property before the sun sets."

When your mom asks why, the farmer tells her spooky story.

Her grandpa had lived with their family on the farm until he died. He was a tireless worker, the first out of the house at sunrise and the last to come in after evening chores. The farmer was thankful for that. But her grandpa was one of the meanest men in the county. He'd take offense and give offense, whatever suited him at the moment. The only thing that seemed to give him pleasure was hunting with his dogs. "They might have been the only creatures who weren't afraid of him," she says. "Which made sense, since Grandpa was the only one who wasn't afraid of them—*and* the only one they obeyed. Without Grandpa's commands, they acted like a wild pack of feral dogs. During hunting season, he and the dogs would disappear for days."

She tells you that when her grandpa wasn't out hunting, fishing, or trapping, he was in his shed. There, he oiled his traps, skinned the animals, and kept to himself. The farmer explains how everyone in the family steered clear of the shed, even the horses. Still, it was the farmer's life, and she got used to a cranky grandpa and scary hunting dogs.

But that's where the story takes a spooky turn.

A year after her grandpa died, his shed burned down. After the flames died down, nothing remained. Her father cleaned the area, raking the shed ashes into the dirt. Strangely, though, even with the shed gone, the horses kicked and reared if anyone walked them near where the shed had been.

"What about his hunting dogs?" you ask. "What happened to them?"

"They kept close to the farm for a while but left one day. Maybe they realized Grandpa wasn't coming back."

She tells you how the farm carried on without her grandpa and the hunting dogs. It was a peaceful place, away from the city noise. The farmer said she thought she'd always live there. Until one night in early fall a few years back.

"What happened?" you ask, detecting a hint of fear in her voice.

The farmer tells you how she and her boyfriend had been sitting outside. It was a perfect night for stargazing. Cool, crisp, and no city lights to cloud the sky. Then, out of nowhere, the smell of a bonfire, earthy and heavy, began to tickle her nose. Soon, she and her boyfriend saw smoke spiraling up into the air, right over the place her grandpa's shed had stood.

"How strange," your mother says. "Who would light a bonfire in the same spot as the hunting shed?"

"There wasn't time to wonder," says the farmer. "Only act." She explains that an untended bonfire can engulf an entire field in minutes. The flames were just a few hundred feet away, so she ran and ran. It seemed like she'd be there in a few steps.

But suddenly . . . the flames disappeared.

"Don't stop!" her boyfriend had shouted. "You're almost there!"

"Where? I don't see them!"

Her boyfriend insisted they were there. "You should see smoke and flames!" He began to call out directions, telling her where to run. "This way, that way. . ."

The farmer crisscrossed the field but couldn't find the fire. She couldn't even see a pile of ashes.

A sense of dread had quickly begun to take over. Standing in the field suddenly seemed like a bad idea. Whatever was lurking, she didn't want to meet it. She raced back to the fence where her boyfriend stood, a bewildered look in his eyes. "Do you hear that sound?" he whispered. "There's something out there."

She did hear something. A fierce and guttural growling. As if a band of wolves or wild dogs were about to attack.

Petrified, the farmer and her boyfriend took off for the house. It was only a few yards away, but they didn't think they would make it. The snarls and howls were right behind them.

Somehow, they got inside safely and managed to bolt the door. All night long, they both kept guard at the kitchen window, watching a pack of dogs circle the house. Teeth bared. Coats bristled. And eyes glowing like burning embers.

"They disappeared at dawn and nobody's seen them since," the farmer says. "That's why I never go back to the farm at night. I don't know where the dogs were from, but I *do* know they weren't of this earth." She hands the bag of tomatoes to your mom. "Anyway." She smiles like she's trying to lighten the mood. "Would you like to see the farm sometime? It really is beautiful this time of year."

You and your mom slowly look up. High above, the skies have turned stormy. The clouds are heavy with rain. It will be dark long before sunset.

You both say, "No," at the same time. This is one invitation to rendezvous with spirits you will happily skip. A human ghost or two? That's fine. A pack of demon dogs? No thanks.

CHAPTER 5

John Boone's Piano

COLUMBIA, MISSOURI

Have you ever heard a song that comes from out of nowhere? It's not an earworm or sticky music—a song that sticks in your head long after you first hear it. This song is coming from outside your head.

You stand still outside the Boone County Historical Society, trying to identify it. It's not a tune you've heard before, but there's still something familiar about it. It's a combination of classical, marching music, and ragtime, the music of the early twentieth century. Its rhythm is offbeat but makes you want to tap your feet and snap your fingers.

You're the only one outside. The guides and visitors left a few minutes ago when your class tour finished. You thought the building was empty. You're waiting for a ride, and you expect to wait awhile. You told your parents the wrong time to pick you up. It's dark and cold—not surprising on a winter night. You wrap your arms around yourself and pace back and forth to keep warm.

Thank goodness for the music.

You listen gratefully. At least it's helping take your mind off the cold. Though it's strangely familiar, it's also different from anything you have heard before.

It's a whirlwind of a tune, beginning with

chime-like tones, almost as if you're sitting in a church. Then there's an explosion of notes that sound like thunder, lightning, then fire bells. Finally, the music slows and lightens. It reminds you of rain dripping from the eaves after a storm.

You remember the tour guide saying, "John Boone was only sixteen years old when a tornado hit Marshfield, Missouri. He never forgot it.

One day, he composed music so the memory would never be lost. The song is called "The Marshfield Tornado." This music *does* sound like a storm, you realize.

But wait—what had the guide said about the piano? It wasn't a player piano, one that plays on its own. Someone or something had to hit the keys. "This is a Chickering piano," the guide had said. "It doesn't look special, does it? There are many pianos, probably prettier than this. But this one belonged to John William Boone, known as John "Blind" Boone, one of the best piano players of his time."

In the moment, you hadn't been all that interested in the tour. In fact, you'd yawned and leaned against a wall. This lecture was going to take a while, you'd thought to yourself. But now, out here in the freezing cold, it's the only thing you can think about to stay warm.

The guide had continued. "John Boone wasn't born blind. He became blind when he was a little boy, after contracting an illness called brain fever, now known as meningitis. The doctors feared his brain might become so swollen it would burst. In those days, one way to relieve pressure on the brain was to remove both of the eyes."

Now the story is getting interesting, you'd thought. *Gross, but interesting.*

"Everyone predicted a sad life for John. He was poor and now blind. What kind of a future would he have?"

The guide had gone on to say it was John's musical talent that saved him. When he was little, he made instruments out of everyday objects. When he got older, he played a harmonica and a tin flute. If he heard a song once, he could replicate it perfectly.

There was something extraordinary about John's music. He couldn't see, but he created music without ever laying eyes on sheet music. His mother's employer heard him play and was so impressed that she told his mother he should go to a school for the blind. She said that John had talent and should be encouraged.

It was at the school that John was introduced to the joy of his life—a piano. "Maybe that's why he pounded the keys," the guide had said. "All that joy pouring out of him?" The guide chuckled. "That's probably why he went through so many pianos in his lifetime."

Sadly, a new director was appointed to the school for the blind. He didn't think it was worthwhile for John to play the piano for a living. He thought John should learn broom-making instead.

John eventually left school, but nothing could stop him from playing. Back home, he became a street performer. One day, a local businessman named John Lange saw him performing. He heard the magic in John's music.

John Lange organized concert tours for John all over the Midwest. John played his heart out, right up to his death at age 63.

When he'd finished with the tale, the guide had smiled. "But that's not the end of the story. That's not why this piano is so special. You see, thirty-three years after his death, John came back . . . for an *encore.*"

Everyone on the tour who had been playing with their phones or whispering to each other stopped.

"Some say John came back because he wanted to revive interest in his music. Locals had been trying to raise money to buy headstones for John and his wife. What if John's music came from 'the other side?' A musician who played from beyond the grave? That would surely catch people's attention."

The guide had then explained that John's encore didn't happen in the Historical Society building. After he died, John's piano was donated to a local school, The Frederick Douglass School. One evening, a woman named Naomi Jones and her daughter Vickie walked by the school on their way home. It was a cold winter day, like today, so they hurried past. But then they heard music playing, and they turned back toward the school.

The music was jazzy, classical and as lively as marching music. The notes flew out the window, strong and sure.

The women were experiencing a personal concert, played for them by John Boone. And it wasn't the only time this happened. They heard John Boone play three more times.

Did these women lead the town effort to raise money for a tombstone for Boone? No one knows. It took eleven more years for the town to raise enough money, the guide had said.

At the end of the tour, you had made your way to the front of the class and examined the piano. Had you seen a key move? *No*, you tell yourself. You only imagined it.

Still, as you wait outside the Historical Society, you wonder if you've just heard the beginning of a performance. Maybe John didn't realize he had an audience waiting for him to play.

Or, maybe he did. Maybe the audience is *you*.

You see your parents' car pulling into the driveway of the Historical Society. As you pick up your backpack, you hear a tin flute play. It peeps out a song you've never heard before. Was this tune coming from John, changing instruments and playing on his tin flute? You listen to a few more notes. The notes are clumsy, forced. No, it's not Blind John. Someone, somewhere, might be trying to play one of his songs. But their music is nothing like that of John Boone's. It couldn't match the mystery and delight of a John Boone masterpiece.

"How was the tour?" your parents ask when you climb into the car.

You shake your head. "Out of this world," you reply.

CHAPTER 6

The Pond

ROCHEPORT, MISSOURI

Some people don't like winter. They bundle up and curse the cold. Some even leave town for warmer places. Not you. You love winter. You can always get warm by layering on more clothes. Besides, if it doesn't get cold, *really* cold, you can't ice skate.

You have a favorite pond not too far from your house. Actually, there are two. One is large and shaped like an hourglass. The other is small and round and very deep. In the summer, you go to watch the herons catch bullfrogs and maybe swim with your friends. But when the pond freezes over, practically all the townspeople come here. The pond is so deep that it's perfect for ice skating. The problem is, that's also what makes the pond so dangerous.

When your parents were trying to warn you about the dangers of the pond, your mom told you a story that got you a little spooked. In the 1930s, a boy drowned here. His family had been skating and decided to go home. But the boy begged to stay and skate alone. What could go wrong? He was a smart boy and a good skater,

and he promised to return home before dark.

But something did go wrong. The boy never returned home. It took hours to find him. He must have skated on thin ice and fallen through. Being alone, there was no one to call for help. The thought makes you shiver a little. But luckily 1930 was a long time ago. Something like that couldn't happen now.

So, there you are, lacing up your skates to get in some skating time before supper. Your friends had to head home to eat with their families, but you don't mind. You promised your parents you wouldn't skate alone, but it's not that big of a deal. You're a good skater. Plus, it's just so much easier when the pond's empty. There's no one to accidentally knock you down or grab you for crack the whip. You *hate* crack the whip. You always seem to get stuck at the end of the skater line, making you the human missile launched when the person next to you drops your hand.

You're so lost in your cheerful thoughts, you don't see the other kid on the ice. You hear him, though. The familiar *scratch scratch* of skates on rough ice makes you look up. There, on the other side of the pond, is someone. Or something. It's hard to tell. It looks like a shadow. You wait for the skater to come closer. Is it one of your friends from school?

But the figure never sharpens. It remains hazy and unformed. You squint your eyes, but all you see is a shadow moving across the ice. Then you hear a frightening sound: ice breaking. Followed by sharp, panicked cries for help. *Oh no!* Shadow or not, you race across the ice. Whoever is there is in trouble. Maybe you can pull the skater out of the water. You just hope the unfortunate person is hanging on to the icy edges of the hole.

A few more glides and you're there, ready to save someone. You've even managed to grab a sturdy branch for the skater to hold on to during the rescue. But . . . there's no hole, no drowning skater. You skate around the pond until the sun goes down, looking for whoever it was. Defeated, confused, and a little bit shaken, you sit on a log and pull off your skates. When you get home, you tell your parents what happened. Instead of being glad you're safe, they're mad.

"You promised you'd come home before dark," your dad lectures. "You could've been hurt."

Your mom asks, "Didn't we tell you? That's why you never go skating alone. You weren't alone, were you?"

Alone.

Her question reminds you of the story they told. About the little boy who fell through the ice and drowned, all those years ago. Suddenly, you feel the hairs on the back of your neck stand up. It was his ghost, you realize. The ghost of the little boy, eternally skating across the pond.

"Well?" your mom asks again.

"No," you answer truthfully. "I wasn't alone."

Chapter 7

University Ghosts

COLUMBIA, MISSOURI

It's fun to live in a college town like Columbia. There's always a game or concert or parade to attend. You like to snooze on the Quad and pretend you're one of the students at the University of Missouri. It's a beautiful spring day and the gardens are popping with pink peonies and purple irises. Still, flowers aren't why you're crossing the campus today. Your parents have been invited to a tea at the

Chancellor's house and you have to go with them. You'd much rather be playing ball, but your dad says the cookies and cakes will be delicious. You figure that desserts are worth spending an hour in a stuffy old house.

He also promises you'll stop at the university's famous granite columns on the way home. They used to adorn the Academic Center. When the building burned down years ago, they were all that remained. Why are they so exciting? Because they're rumored to have bloodstains on them, left there after a murder in 1853. Lately, you and your friends have been daring each other to visit the columns after midnight. One of them even researched the columns to find out who killed whom, and when and why.

William Thornton and Benjamin Handy, your friend reports, were once great friends.

When they didn't want to study or go to class, they often played cards. One night, though, the friendship ended.

William Thornton accused Benjamin Handy of cheating. The two argued but eventually went to bed. Unfortunately, a night's sleep didn't calm down either one. The next morning at breakfast, Thornton called out Handy, saying he had tricked him the night before. This time, they came to blows. Other students pulled them apart and the fight finished. But not for long.

Most everyone thought William and Benjamin would eventually forget their argument and move on. When the college suspended William for starting the fight, their friends assumed time off from school would make him think twice about ever starting another one.

But Benjamin Handy didn't think the fight was over. He bought a cane and bragged to friends that he'd whip Thornton with it the next time he saw him. He also bought a bowie knife, a large blade used for hand-to-hand combat—not hunting.

A mutual friend arranged a meeting to encourage the pair to make peace. The two resumed their studies and things were quiet for a while. But a few days before Christmas, the truce ended. It was Handy who made the first move. After class, he attacked Thornton and pinned him to a wall. During the struggle, Thornton pulled out a pistol and killed Handy.

It wasn't the only deadly shooting at the Academic Building. Years later, a university professor shot and killed a student in self-defense. Not much is known about this killing, but people say it left a stain on the columns.

More than 150 years later, the columns still stand. Since the 1970s, there have been reports of ghostly figures solidifying into shadows of men. You and your friends have tried again and again to see the hauntings, but so far, you've been unlucky. Still, you've heard others describe the man-shaped shadows, drifting away from the columns toward town like a fog. Some say the shapes solidify the moment they leave campus grounds.

You and your friends have tried again and again to see the hauntings, but so far you've been unlucky. There's another reason you've agreed to go to the Chancellor's house for tea—you might just see spooks. Unlike the hauntings at the columns, *this* ghost was never angry at anyone. In fact, you've heard the spirit of Alice Read seemed more concerned with keeping the electricity bill down and nosey visitors out of private areas.

According to local legend, Alice Read arrived at the Chancellor's house when her husband Daniel became the new president of the University of Missouri. His new role meant long hours, many meetings, and lots of work. However, it also meant living in a beautiful mansion.

Daniel Read was said to have been popular among the students. He opened the university to women in the 1860s, a time when many universities only admitted men. He and his wife, Alice, hosted countless dinners and parties for students and professors. In fact, the family was so well regarded that when the university built a lake on campus, the faculty and students named it after their daughter, Mary.

Maybe that's why Alice doesn't want to leave her house. Where else could she have been happier than her time at the University of Missouri?

Alice died in 1874. She stayed away for sixteen years, then suddenly returned to haunt the mansion. Strange lights and shadowy figures floated inside and out. People were so convinced burglars were trying to break in that the school assigned a security guard to watch the house.

Perhaps the guards calmed Alice, because she wasn't seen again until 1994. Richard Wallace, a new college president, moved in that year with his family.

At first, they loved all the old furniture that had been left behind. The chiming of the grandfather clock charmed them . . . until they discovered the clock didn't have any working mechanisms. Then came the strange crashing sounds from the attic, even though the attic was almost entirely empty. Objects in the house moved from place to place without any help from human hands. And shadowy figures seemed to waltz in the windows, as if dancing to ghostly music. Still, no one took the hauntings seriously.

"I hope we get a tour of the house," says your mom. She likes ghosts, too. "Alice Read is supposed to hang out on the third floor. That's where the attic is."

"Have you seen her?" you ask.

"Not yet."

After you and the other visitors walk

through the front door, you purposely drop to the back of the group. There are a lot of people, so it's easy for you to break off and slide into a dark corner.

You wait until the last person walks into the front room, then you dash up the stairs. You peek into the bedrooms on the second floor, but there's nothing but furniture. You're a bit nervous as you climb the steps to the third floor. All you see are a few empty rooms and an entryway to what you think is a storage closet. There's something odd about it. A decorative grille seals it off from the rest of the hallway. Was someone trying to keep people out ... or something else in? You turn the doorknob, just so you can peek.

That's when you hear a *swish*, like the sound of a silk or satin dress. There's a spark of light from the room. You can see it! Then, suddenly, the doorknob is yanked from your hand. You feel a great gust of wind as the door slams in front of you. A second later, you are tearing down the stairs and out of the house as fast as you possibly can.

Luckily, you don't have to wait long for your parents. Maybe the owners heard the attic door slam and knew someone was snooping. Perhaps they decided to let Alice relax and enjoy her home without so many nosey guests.

When your parents join you a few minutes later, they say the visit was cut short. Not because anyone heard a door slam ... but because the lights in the front room kept flickering on and off.

"I'm glad you weren't there," says your dad.

"It spooked a lot of people." He frowns. "By the way, where *were* you?"

Your mom gives you a pointed look. "I think you had your own spooky experience. Am I right?"

So, she *had* heard the door slam.

You nod yes, grateful that instead of scolding you for exploring the house on your own, she simply hands you a gooey, gourmet-looking cookie.

"Alice wanted you to have it," she says with a wink.

"Haha," you say. But when you take a bite, it really is one of the best cookies you've ever tasted.

"Well?" your dad says. "How is it?"

"Spectacular," you reply.

Or should you say . . . *spooktacular*?

CHAPTER 8

Lilac Hill

FAYETTE, MISSOURI

In the old days, it was common for extended families to live together. You might share your home with a widowed grandmother, a good-for-nothing uncle, or an unmarried cousin. Sometimes the relative was helpful—a pleasure to spend time with. But other times, the relation was a problem.

Even *after* they passed away.

After all, it's one thing to put up with an annoying cousin when she's alive. But just imagine if you had to put up with her after she's dead and buried! The unmarried cousin at Lilac Hill was one such pest.

You're glad you're visiting Lilac Hill. It's a red brick plantation house with columns lining the front porch. It's especially beautiful in the spring, when ancient lilac bushes fill the air with an intense, syrupy sweetness that you like (but makes your dad sneeze). "Those flowers sure are strong," he says with a sniff.

Your parents start shushing as soon as you walk through the door. "We're just visiting for a little bit to welcome our friends to Missouri," they say. "Behave."

You sigh. Ever since the incident in Alice Read's attic at the University of Missouri, they treat you like a little kid who can't be trusted. "I will, I will," you grumble. But the truth is, you'd *love* to explore this place without them hovering. Lilac Hill is known to be a little spooky. Your parents' old friends have just moved in, so hopefully they'll talk for a while and you can look around.

Inside, Lilac Hill looks like a museum. Hand-carved wooden trim decorates most of the rooms. Windows shaped like sunbursts perch over the doorways. You notice there are two chimneys and lots of fireplaces. You stand in the middle of the dining room, afraid to move and break one of the porcelain figurines on a side table.

"Be careful!" warns the housekeeper.

"I'm not going to break anything," you protest.

"It's not you," she replies. "It's Aunt Minnie. She's very particular about guests."

"Aunt Minnie?" you say. "Who's that?"

The housekeeper pulls out two chairs and invites you to sit. She tells you all about the history of Lilac Hill ... and the woman who once called it home. "Alfred Morrison built Lilac Hill in the late 1800s. He had prospered as a farmer and a politician and wanted a house that displayed his success. When he died, he passed the house on to his son James. James was known to have a tender heart, so no one was surprised when he invited his unmarried cousin Minnie to live with him. The mansion had so many rooms, why not share some of the wealth?"

"That was nice of him," you say. "She must have been pretty grateful."

"Minnie made her mark from the start," the housekeeper goes on. "Few in town liked her. They might be able to put up with her prim and proper ways, but no one could sit and listen to her opinions on everything. One of her favorite topics was women with bad reputations. She never explained what a bad reputation meant. She just decided whether or not a lady—or anyone, for that matter—was good enough to come into their house."

"Oh," you say. "Wow." Your eyes dart around the room. You wonder what Minnie would think about *you* being in her house.

"Mm-hm." The housekeeper nods. "Imagine, then, how Minnie reacted when her cousin James got married to someone whose husband had died. Someone must have told Minnie that James's bride was not a proper lady, so when he brought her home, trouble really started. Life at Lilac Hill changed—and not for the better. As the original lady of the house, Minnie wanted her way and *wasn't* happy when she didn't get it."

"What happened?" you ask.

"Well, Lilac Hill must have seen more than a few arguments, cold shoulders, and silent treatments," she says. "But when she eventually died, things got even worse! For years, people say Aunt Minnie's ghost made her cousin and his wife miserable. Spooking them, scaring them, slamming around in the attic late at night so they couldn't sleep, that kind of thing." The housekeeper sighs. "Still, the house persevered, even after James and his wife died. Years passed, but it quickly became apparent that Minnie's spirit had *not*. She had laid her claim to Lilac Hill and wasn't going to give it up to anyone—even from beyond the grave."

The housekeeper excuses herself and goes to make some tea. When she returns, she serves cookies and sugary, milky chamomile, just the way you like it.

"Are you scared of Minnie?" you ask. "She doesn't sound like a very . . . friendly ghost."

"I'm the only housekeeper who's *not* afraid of Minnie." She takes a sip of tea. "I'm not afraid of any old lady, even if she is a ghost. Your family's friends who bought the house had a bit of a rough start, but I think they're used to Minnie now."

She keeps on with the story.

"The first weeks were quiet, and everyone wondered if Minnie had moved on. Then the wailing began. It started in the middle of the night and was loud enough to wake up the entire family. I helped check all the bedrooms, thinking one of the kids was upset, but we never found the source of the crying. After a while, we all realized the noises only happen in a few of the rooms. Once you shut the door, the crying stops."

You take a deep breath. "I'm glad *I* don't have to sleep here," you say.

"That hasn't been the only disturbance," she says. "We figured out the attic is at the heart of the trouble. Sometimes you can hear heavy objects being dragged and dropped across the floor."

You frown. "Why do you think Aunt Minnie's so upset?"

"She must not have been getting enough attention all these years," the housekeeper explains. "She started turning on water faucets. Once the bathroom sink overflowed, flooding the first floor! It's happened a few times, even though nobody's turned on the water. I've even called a plumber to check all the pipes, every one of them."

"Does . . . *he* think it's a ghost?"

She nods. "That's what he said."

"Have *you* ever seen Aunt Minnie?" you have to ask.

"Not personally. But once, there were some farmers hauling hay nearby. It must have been a hot day, because they decided to get some water from one of the outside water pumps. No sooner had they each taken a drink than an old lady burst from the faucet and chased them away." She shakes her head. "I always know when she's nearby, though. The air always turns sweet. Almost . . . syrupy sweet. Apparently, when she was alive, Minnie loved perfume."

Your eyes go wide. You remember the strong scent outside. How your dad was sneezing on the porch. Is it possible it wasn't the lilac bushes . . . but Aunt Minnie's perfume?

That night, when you get home, you do your

own research. You want to figure out why Aunt Minnie can't move on. And what's causing her to cry at night.

According to the newspapers, an old tombstone was found in one of the Lilac Hill sheds. Surprisingly, it was missing an inscription. Could the grave marker have been meant for Minnie? Maybe she's crying because she was buried without it? Then you read about other scary things that happened in the house. Like in 1853, when two of the family's children died within days of each other, possibly because they were *poisoned*. And how once, during a renovation in the basement, they found wrist chains attached to the walls. Could someone have been held there? Someone who might still be calling for help? You close your computer. Both of those stories are enough to keep *you* from sleeping, too.

In the end, you decide whatever happened to Aunt Minnie, she's stayed in the house for at least one main reason: even hundreds of years later, she still thinks *she* is the only one worthy to be there. She was a prim and proper lady, after all.

CHAPTER 9

John Neihardt and the Ghosts of Skyrim

SKYRIM, MISSOURI

Why oh why? you ask yourself. *Why am I here again?* How many field trips does a kid have to go on to the same place? You're back at the Boone County Historical Society. You check the time on your phone and sigh. There's still an hour to go. You follow your class into the art gallery, staying in the very back so at least you don't have to listen to the guide.

The guide is pointing out paintings by George Caleb Bingham. He says, "More than any other artist, George Caleb Bingham captured nineteenth-century life on the Missouri River."

That's all you hear. You've suddenly noticed a statue of an old man with an impressive head of hair. You know the statue is called a bust, a replica of someone's head. And you know it's just a piece of clay. But there's something about this statue that makes it hard to look away. It's so . . . *alive*.

"That's John Neihardt," says a voice behind you. When you turn, you see a woman you don't recognize. "Look at that hair!" she says. "Whenever he crossed the campus, people knew who he was before he came within one hundred feet." The lady sighs a little sadly. "Sometimes I think people remember him for his hair, not the work he did with paranormal research."

Paranormal research? You know all about that! "You mean night cameras, EVPs and K-2 meters?" you ask. You can hardly contain your excitement.

"Those tools came long after his time." The woman laughs. "John Neihardt had to rely on séances."

Séances? You picture a dark room with levitating tables and, if he was lucky, a ghost speaking through a live medium.

She nods. "That's all he had to communicate with the spirits."

For a second, you consider catching up with your class. But this lady, even if she is a bit odd is talking about ghosts. And you *love* ghosts.

She must know you are interested, because when she sits down on a museum bench, she waves you over to sit next to her. She starts to tell you a story.

"Ever since he was a boy, John Neihardt believed there was a world other than the one we live in. Once, after suffering from a high fever, he had a dream—or some would say, a hallucination. He saw himself in the air, flying, racing to get somewhere. He was in a rush because he thought everything would end when the black curtain fell."

She looks to see if you are still listening. (You are.)

"After, he was convinced that even when we die, and our body deteriorates, our individual intelligence remains. That, and the time he spent with an Oglala Lakota holy man named Black Elk, learning the Lakota stories and beliefs, made him certain that the world we live in is not the only world.

You nod. Your history teacher had told you all about the book Neihardt had written even though you'd forgotten his name. So, it *was* this old man with the bushy hair who wrote about the spirit world of the Oglala Lakota people!

"That's why John Neihardt insisted on round tables for his séances," she says. "He was honoring the Oglala Lakota belief in the power of circles."

"I'd like to go to one," you tell her.

"Only if you really wanted to connect with the spirit world," she says. "John insisted on that. If the people seated around the table didn't believe, there could be no communication. The spirit world needed the combined power of everyone to move objects in *our* world."

"What happened at the séances?" you ask.

The lady sits up, almost as if she's about

to brag. "A doll levitated, a metal tray floated, and once, a tray cartwheeled out the door into the garden!"

"*Wow*," you say. You are hooked.

"John died in 1973," the woman explains. "Or at least, his *body* did. One of his daughters sold her home, which her father visited frequently. Luckily, the new owners weren't frightened by his visits."

"Visits?" you ask. "What do you mean?"

"At first," she says, "when the lights flickered on and off for no reason, the family chuckled. But they *did* have a problem with the midnight visits. One of their sons reported that an old man with white bushy hair would stand at the foot of his bed. The man never spoke a word, just stared. As I remember, when the son visits now, even as an adult, he refuses to sleep in that room."

"He must have had a nightmare," you say. You spot your classmates and wonder if you should join them again. For some reason, her story suddenly has you feeling a little spooked.

The lady cocks an eyebrow. "What if the spirit visits during the daytime?"

You sit back on the bench. You're starting to wonder how she knows so much about John Neihardt.

"I was close to John's family," she says, almost as if she's read your mind. "Very close. I spent a lot of time in their home at Skyrim Farm. One of the things we liked to do was ride horses on the property. One day, my horse spooked and I almost fell off. I'll never forget what my friend told me that day, when I asked if there had been anything that could have spooked the horse."

You swallow. "What did she say?"

The woman leans closer, lowering her voice.

"She said it was a *spirit*. She told me there were *lots* of spirits on the property, and they liked to be out in the sunshine, just like we do. She figured one of them must have crossed in front of my horse."

"Did you . . . believe her?" you ask.

"Of course!" she exclaims. "I know all about the Neihardt family." She walks over to the bust of John Neihardt and poses next to it. When her bushy white hair brushes up against the statue's, she laughs. "See the family resemblance?"

Looking closely, you notice they share similar facial features. The same nose shape and the same wild white hair. But then you freeze. Did you just see the statue . . . smile?

Suddenly, a museum guard steps over. "No touching the exhibits," he scolds. "Time to move on."

That's a command you can obey. The lady—and this statue—are getting a little too spooky for you. You say a quick goodbye, step back, then run to catch up with your classmates. When you look back over your shoulder, the woman has vanished. Almost like she was never there at all.

That night, you can't stop thinking about the woman at the museum. Had she really been related to John Neihardt? If so, did she truly believe in the paranormal? And did you imagine it . . . or did the statue *actually* smile at you? You'll never know.

CHAPTER 10

Ravenswood Mansion

BUNCETON, MISSOURI

Today is your lucky day. After weeks and weeks of waiting for an invitation, you get to be a ghost hunter! Maybe it's because you begged to go along with the local paranormal society on their investigation. You've heard Ravenswood mansion is a hot spot and you're finally getting to see it for yourself.

As you help lug the ghost hunting equipment to the car, you wonder if the ghost hunting society only needs your muscles, not your eyes and ears. The night vision cameras, K-2 meters, and EVPs—all special tools used for hunting ghosts and detecting paranormal activity—are heavy. Still, you're excited to try them out and see what kind of spooky stuff they'll help you discover around town.

The EVP recorders capture sounds that can't be heard with a human ear. Whether the sounds are whispers, voices, or any kind of noise at all, the EVP recorder will catch them. Night vision cameras let you capture video on the darkest night, inside or outside. The K-2 meter is an electromagnetic meter that measures electromagnetic energy. Ghosts and spirits are said to disrupt the electromagnetic field, and that's what the K-2 will tell you.

When the car pulls up to the house, you understand why people think it's haunted. Ravenswood is set on eighty acres out in the country. *It must be lonely out here*, you think. It must have been hard to get people to visit. It's so far away from everything.

Still, it's as pretty as everyone says it is. The red brick mansion is two-and-a-half stories tall with grand columns lining its front porch. Everyone agreed Nathaniel Leonard had built a beauty. When his son Charles inherited Ravenswood, he added to the mansion, inside and out. He and his wife Nadine traveled the world and brought back souvenirs, including a sixteenth-century suit of armor and European bronzes. The home was a showcase of the latest and finest for the time.

The credit for this went to Nadine. Not only did she love the finer things, she loved to show them off with parties. In the summer months, she'd have the servants string Japanese paper lanterns across the lawns. Guests danced to live orchestra music. Nadine must have enjoyed every moment. Is it surprising to think that when Nadine died, perhaps her spirit decided to stick around? Why go anywhere when you have everything you want at home?

Your ghost hunting group splits up into teams. The first team, including you, moves to the dining room, where Nadine had countless elegant dinner parties. "Let's reenact a party," one of the ladies says. "Nadine loved to entertain."

She closes her eyes for a moment, turning serious and focused, then clearly and calmly asks Nadine if she'd like to join them. That's when the fun starts.

Another investigator asks, "Is Ravenswood haunted by real spirits? Or perhaps there's a residual presence here?" She turns to you and explains,

"That's when a place holds on to the energy of the people who lived there."

Your group listens and waits for a minute or two, but nothing happens. Did that question insult Nadine? Does she think she is much more than a residual presence?

Maybe *that's* why the K-2 meter suddenly flashes from green to red.

"Oh!" you cry out. You feel a wave of static electricity wash over you. It rolls through your body, head to toe, and the surge makes your hair stand on end.

Whoa.

Now that things are happening, you all decide to stay longer. You hope you'll get another interesting reading from the K-2 meter, and before you know it, you do! The K-2 meter surges from green to red all over again, and this time, you *all* feel the wave of static electricity. That's when you hear an unearthly sound from the second floor.

You decide to investigate.

As you climb the grand staircase, you feel another bolt of electricity. This time, though, it's much stronger. Looking around, you see that everyone has experienced it.

"The house is active tonight," says the group leader. "Maybe we'll see Nadine. She's made herself known a number of times in the past. Why not tonight, too?"

You decide to spread out, with some heading to Nadine's room and others checking out the hallway.

Feeling brave, you join the others in trying to contact Nadine. "Show yourself, Nadine!" you call out. Everyone is so on edge, your whole group jumps when there's a noise—a bang so loud and intense it seems to shake the house.

You race back down the staircase toward the sound, but you don't find a thing. You notice the air has turned chilly, like somebody's opened a window. Something is definitely happening in this house. Slowly, you head back upstairs. You open the door to Nadine's room, flinching when it creaks. This time, you hear a *knock knock* on one of the bedroom walls. But when you go in to investigate, you again find nothing. One by one, you explore every bedroom upstairs, and each time you hear the same mysterious knocks. By now you are feeling *seriously* spooked.

Eventually, the knocks shift back out into the hallway. Now it sounds like old pieces of ceiling plaster falling on the stairs. But just like before, when you examine the ceiling, you see no evidence of damage.

The knocks continue, traveling deeper into

the house. Where are they leading you? The pops and bangs move up to the third floor. Now you hear footsteps, *lots* of them. Your heart is beating fast. You wonder if the ghost is teasing you, because when you climb the attic stairs, the noises and footsteps stop.

After what seems like hours of playing Nadine's ghostly game, your group decides to end the investigation. You're exhausted from chasing the bangs and pops and footfalls. Except for the crazy readings from the K-2 meter, you have no proof that it really is Nadine haunting the house.

Later, though, you hear something that sends a chill straight up your spine. It comes from the EVP recorder you listen to after you leave the house. Investigators usually review EVP tapes after they finish an investigation, because there's no time to do it during a search. You press play and listen hard. There it is. Seconds after you call out to Nadine, you hear a faint but undeniable voice.

A woman's voice.

And she does *not* sound happy.

"*Hushhhhh....*"

You decide it has to be Nadine. She was such an elegant lady, used to throwing lavish parties and living a life of riches. She must have been annoyed to have your group peeking into her rooms and clattering up and down her grand staircase. You hadn't been formally invited, after all.

A Ghostly Goodbye

People say there are good reasons Columbia is home to so many ghosts. Two mighty rivers—the Missouri and the Mississippi—run through the state. Natural springs, rolling hills, deep ravines, and caves dot the landscape, and limestone lies below. These are the perfect conditions for spirits, paranormal investigators say.

In fact, it seems there have always been spirits in Missouri. Indigenous peoples spoke of ghosts, both good and bad, who return from the dead. The early farmers added their own ghostly tales when they settled in the state. So, when you visit Columbia, Missouri, expect to see more than gently rolling hills and mighty rivers. You'll see pretty towns, lively museums, and college life. And if you're lucky, you'll meet a few ghosts, too.

Karen Emily Miller has been writing about strange creatures since she was six years old, so writing about the paranormal is a perfect fit. She just moved to Iowa City and is excited to meet new ghosts there.

Check out some of the other *Spooky America* titles available now!

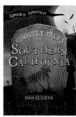

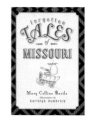

Spooky America was adapted from the creeptastic *Haunted America* series for adults. *Haunted America* explores historical haunts in cities and regions across America. Here's more from the original *Haunted Columbia, Missouri* author Mary Collins Barile: